G. MacCallum.

The Life of
St Andrew

Anita Ganeri

Heinemann
LIBRARY

www.heinemann.co.uk/library
Visit our website to find out more information about **Heinemann Library** books.

To order:

 Phone 44 (0) 1865 888066

 Send a fax to 44 (0) 1865 314091

 Visit the Heinemann Bookshop at www.heinemann.co.uk/library to browse our catalogue and order online.

First published in Great Britain by Heinemann Library, Halley Court, Jordan Hill, Oxford OX2 8EJ, part of Harcourt Education.
Heinemann is a registered trademark of Harcourt Education Ltd.

Editorial: Lucy Thunder and Helen Cannons
Design: Richard Parker and Tinstar Design Ltd.
(www.tinstar.co.uk)
Illustrations: Mike Lacey
Picture Research: Rebecca Sodergren and Liz Moore
Production: Edward Moore

Originated by Repro Multi-Warna
Printed and bound in China by South China Printing Company
The paper used to print this book comes from sustainable resources.

ISBN 0 431 18084 9
08 07 06 05 04
10 9 8 7 6 5 4 3 2 1

British Library Cataloguing in Publication Data
Anita Ganeri
The Life of St Andrew. – (Life of saints)
271.1'092
A full catalogue record for this book is available from the British Library.

Acknowledgements
The publishers would like to thank the following for permission to reproduce photographs: Art Archive/San Apollinare Nuovo Ravenna/Dagli Orti (A) p 8; The Bridgeman Art Library/State Russian Museum, St Petersburg p12; Collections/Archie Young pp 20, 21; Corbis/Kelly-Mooney Photography p 4; Corbis/John & Lisa Merrill p 22; E & E Picture Library/Anson p 17; Sonia Halliday Photographs p 5, 6; Sonia Halliday & Laura Lushington p 11; Robert Harding Picture Library/Nigel Francis p 26; Historic Scotland pp 19, 23; The Image Bank p 24; Still Moving Pictures Co/Andrea Cringean p 27; Topham Picturepoint p 9; Trip/D. Hastilow p 14; Trip/H. Rogers p 10; Trip/B. Turner p 18.

Cover photograph of St Andrew, on a stained-glass window in the Church of St Neot, Cornwall, reproduced with permission of Sonia Halliday Photographs and Laura Lushington.

The publishers would like to thank Fr. Martin Ganeri OP for his assistance in the preparation of this book.

Contents

Words shown in the text in bold, **like this**, are explained in the glossary.

What is a saint?

In the **Christian** religion, people try to live a **holy** life. Some men and women are especially holy. The Christian Church calls them saints. Christians believe that saints are very close to God.

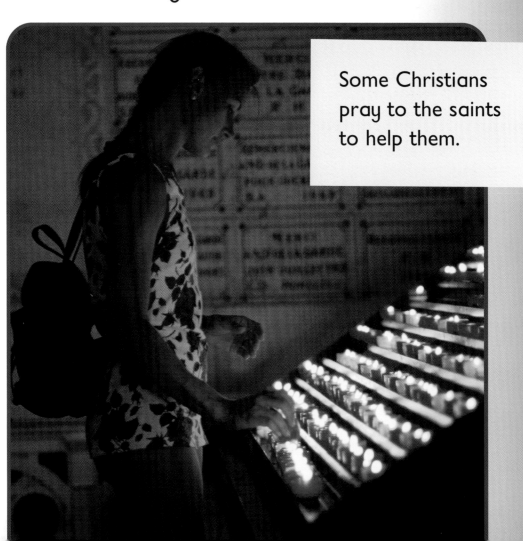

Some Christians pray to the saints to help them.

Some saints look after a country or a group of people, such as doctors or travellers. They are called **patron saints**. This book is about St Andrew, the patron saint of Scotland.

St Andrew is often shown as an old man holding a cross, and a book or a fishing net.

St Andrew's early life

Andrew was born about 2000 years ago in Galilee, **Palestine**. We do not know much for certain about Andrew's life. Most of our information comes from legends and stories.

The Sea of Galilee, in Israel, today.

Andrew's father was a fisherman. Andrew and his brother, Simon, became fishermen like him. Every day, they sailed out in their boats to catch fish in the Sea of Galilee.

So many fish

The **Bible** tells how, one day, **Jesus** came to Galilee. He saw Andrew and Simon pulling in their nets. Although they had been working all night, they had not caught a single fish.

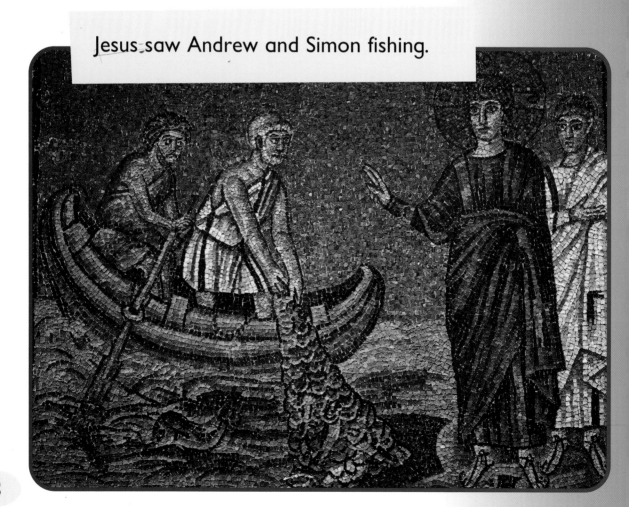

Jesus saw Andrew and Simon fishing.

Jesus told them to throw their nets into deeper water. This time, they caught so many fish that their nets nearly broke. Then Jesus asked Andrew and Simon to become his **disciples**.

Jesus is shown here with Andrew, Simon and the other ten disciples.

Loaves and fishes

Andrew and the other **disciples** travelled around **Palestine** with **Jesus**. They helped him to teach people about God. One day, a huge crowd of people came to listen to Jesus.

Jesus teaching the crowd of five thousand people.

It was late and people were hungry. Andrew saw a boy who had five loaves and two small fishes. He took them to Jesus. Jesus turned them into enough food for everyone to eat.

The crowd were amazed at what Jesus had done.

Andrew goes on his travels

A few years later, **Jesus** died. Andrew left **Palestine** and travelled far and wide. He made several trips to Greece. He may also have visited Turkey, Russia and Poland.

This painting of St Andrew was made in Russia, where Andrew is an important saint.

Everywhere Andrew went, he tried to teach people about being a **Christian**. Many people came to hear him speak. Some of them became Christians after hearing him teach.

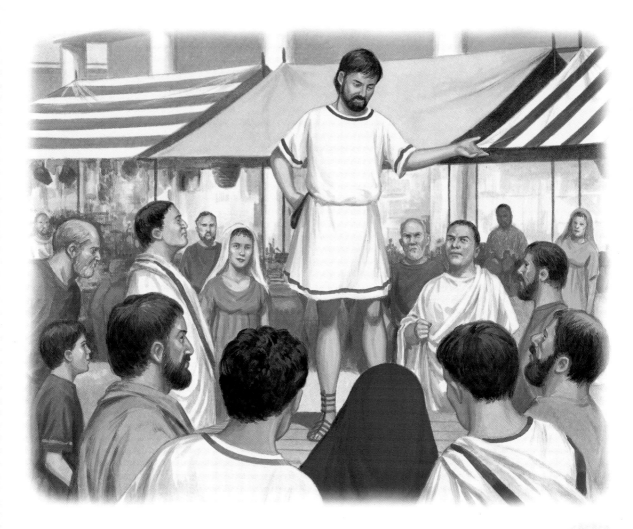

Healing the sick

Andrew was a kind and **holy** man. On his last journey to Greece, he visited a city called Patras. Many sick people came to see him and Andrew helped to make them better.

This is the city of Patras in southern Greece.

In those days, Greece was ruled by the Romans. Andrew healed a woman called Maximillia. She was the wife of a powerful Roman **general** and she became a **Christian**.

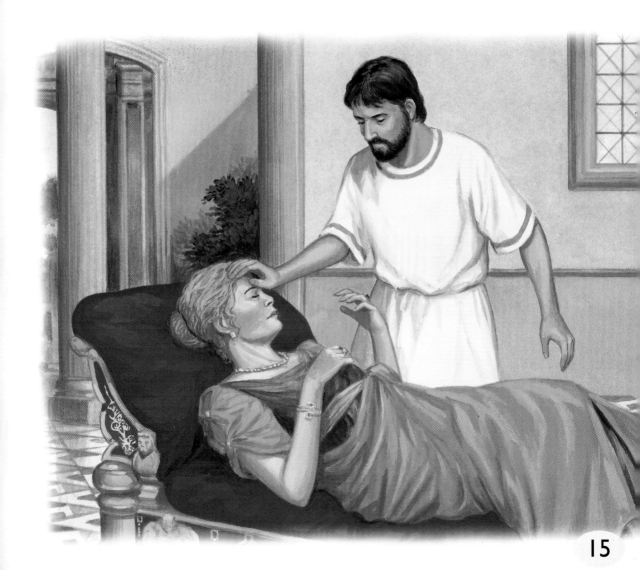

Andrew dies

The Roman **general** was angry that his wife had become a **Christian**. He wanted to stop the new religion. So he ordered his soldiers to put Andrew to death.

Andrew was **crucified** in about AD 60. He asked to die on an X-shaped cross. He said he was not good enough to die on an upright cross like **Jesus** had.

The shape of the cross shown is called the cross of St Andrew.

A monk to the rescue

After his death, Andrew was buried in a **tomb** in Patras, Greece. But 300 years later, a Roman **emperor** wanted to move the bones and bury them in a new church in Turkey.

Emperor Constantine wanted to move Andrew's bones to Turkey.

At that time, a Greek **monk** called Regulus had a strange dream. An angel told him to rescue some of the bones and take them far away, for safety.

This tower in the Scottish town of St Andrews is named after St Regulus. He was also called St Rule.

Andrew of Scotland

The story goes that Regulus took some of Andrew's bones and sailed away with them. After a long and stormy journey, his ship was wrecked off the east coast of Scotland.

This is the east coast of Scotland at St Andrews. Regulus came ashore here.

Here Regulus built a **chapel** where the bones were kept. Andrew never visited Scotland when he was alive. But this is one story of how he became Scotland's **patron saint**.

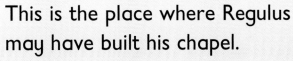
This is the place where Regulus may have built his chapel.

The bishop's bones

Another story tells that later some of Andrew's bones were taken to Rome, in Italy. A **bishop** from Britain visited Rome and brought some of the bones back to Scotland.

Many people think that Andrew's bones came to Scotland from Rome, in Italy.

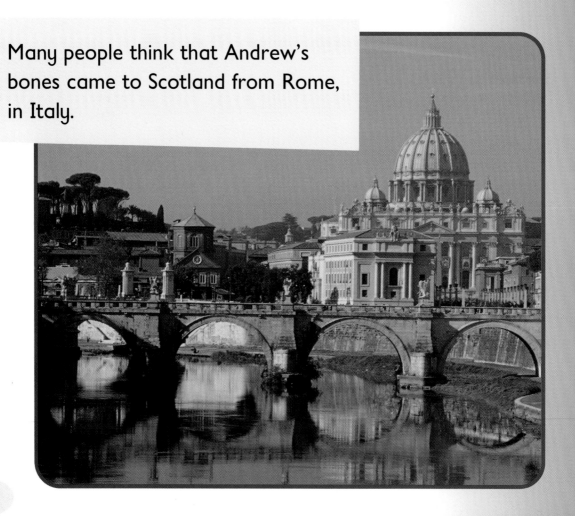

The bishop put the bones in a **chapel** in the town of St Andrews. Visitors flocked to see the bones. They believed that the bones had special powers.

This painting shows pilgrims on their way to see St Andrew's bones.

Flags and battles

You can see the cross of St Andrew on the flag of Scotland. Legend says that, hundreds of years ago, King Angus of Scotland prayed to St Andrew to help him in battle.

The flag of Scotland shows the white cross of St Andrew on a blue background.

In a dream, St Andrew told the king that he would help. On the day of battle, King Angus saw a white cross in the blue sky. This was a sign that the king would win the battle.

St Andrew's Day

On 30 November, people all over the world celebrate St Andrew's Day. To celebrate, there is **bagpipe** music, singing and Scottish dancing.

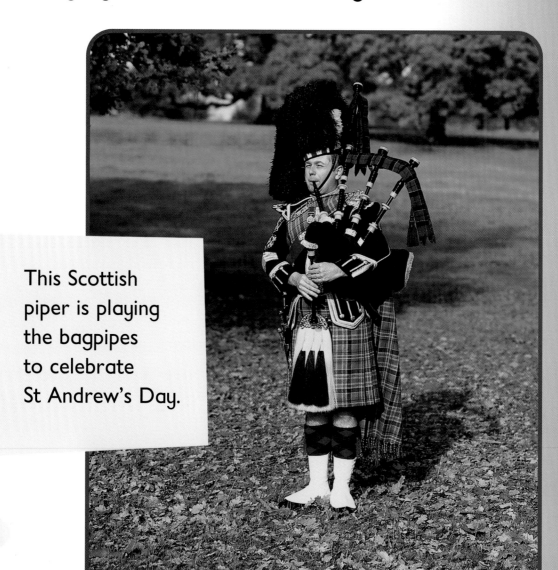

This Scottish piper is playing the bagpipes to celebrate St Andrew's Day.

There is also a special dinner to mark St Andrew's Day. People eat traditional Scottish food, such as **cock-a-leekie** soup, **haggis** and oatcakes.

Many people eat haggis to celebrate St Andrew's Day. This man is cutting the haggis.

 **Fact file**

■ In pictures and statues, St Andrew is usually shown as an old man with a long beard, holding an X-shaped cross, a book and sometimes a fishing net.

■ Andrew was one of the twelve **disciples**. They were **Jesus**'s closest friends and followers. They taught people about Jesus after his death.

■ St Andrew is also the **patron saint** of Russia, Greece, fishermen, singers and women who have not got married.

■ The bones Regulus brought to Scotland are thought to have been an arm bone, a kneecap and some fingerbones.

■ A piece of wood believed to come from St Andrew's cross can be seen in an abbey in Marseilles, France.

Timeline

We do not know for certain when St Andrew was born or died. You can use the dates below as a guide.

- **Around AD 5** St Andrew is born in Palestine
- **Around 27** St Andrew becomes a disciple of Jesus
- **Around 30** St Andrew begins to travel and teach people about Jesus
- **Around 60** St Andrew is **crucified**
- **Around 357 Emperor** Constantine moves St Andrew's bones from Greece to Turkey
- **Around 369** Some people think Regulus brings some of St Andrew's bones to Scotland. Andrew becomes patron saint of Scotland.
- **Around 733** Other people think the Bishop of Hexham brings some of St Andrew's bones to Scotland
- **Around 832** King Angus wins the Battle of Athelstaneford, after praying to St Andrew
- **1160** St Andrew's **Cathedral** is built

Glossary

AD way of counting dates, starting from year zero

bagpipes musical instrument

Bible the Christians' holy book

bishop leader in the Christian Church

cathedral large church

chapel small church or part of a church

Christian follower of the teachings of Jesus Christ

cock-a-leekie soup made from chicken, leeks and prunes

crucified killed by being nailed to a cross

disciples special friends or followers of Jesus

emperor the ruler of the Roman Empire

general important soldier

haggis special meat dish eaten in Scotland

holy to do with God

Jesus a teacher who lived about 2000 years ago. Christians believe he was the son of God.

monk man who belongs to a special religious group

Palestine ancient Middle Eastern country

patron saint saint who has a special interest in a country or group of people

tomb place where a dead person is buried

Find out more

Books

Celebrations!: Christmas, Jennifer Gillis (Raintree, 2003)

Places of Worship: Catholic Churches, Clare Richards (Heinemann Library, 1999)

Places of Worship: Protestant Churches, Mandy Ross (Heinemann Library, 1999)

Websites

www.britainexpress.com
Information about different parts of Britain, the history of Britain and famous people, including saints.

www.saint-andrewsday.com
Information about St Andrew and about how St Andrew's Day is celebrated.

Index

Titles in *The Life of* series include:

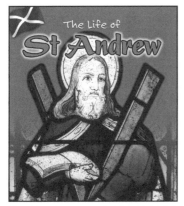

Hardback   0 431 18084 9

Hardback   0 431 18081 4

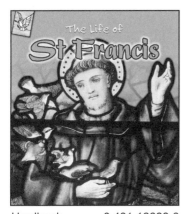

Hardback   0 431 18080 6

Hardback   0 431 18082 2

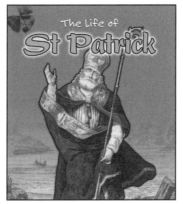

Hardback   0 431 18083 0

Find out about the other titles in this series on our website www.heinemann.co.uk/library